SPIN!

Grammar, Vocabulary, and Writing

D

Diane Pinkley

Genevieve J. Kocienda

Contributing Writer: Barbara Barysh

Longman

Spin! D

Pearson Education, 10 Bank Street, White Plains, NY 10606

Vice president, director of instructional design: Allen Ascher
Executive editor: Anne Stribling
Senior development editor: Barbara Barysh
Vice president, director of design and production: Rhea Banker
Executive managing editor: Linda Moser
Production manager: Liza Pleva
Production editor: Sasha Kintzler
Art director: Patricia Wosczyk
Director of manufacturing: Patrice Fraccio
Senior manufacturing buyer: Edith Pullman
Cover design: Elizabeth Carlson
Cover art: Mary Jane Begin
Cover photo: © Masterfile
Text design: Patricia Wosczyk
Text composition: TSI Graphics
Text art: Jerry Zimmerman

ISBN: 0-13-041994-X

2 3 4 5 6 7 8 9 10—WC—08 07 06 05 04 03

Contents

Ordinal Numbers 2
Prepositions of Time: *in, on, at* 3
Past Tense: *was* 3
Quantities 6
Hello! 7

UNIT **1** All About Us 9
Adjectives 10
Comparative Adjectives: *-er* 11
Time Clause: *when* 13
Writing Sentences: *and, but* 14

UNIT **2** Last Weekend 17
Past Tense: Regular Verbs 18
Past Tense: Irregular Verbs 19
before/after 21
Writing Sentences: *or* 22
REVIEW: UNITS 1 AND 2 25

UNIT **3** Let's Eat 27
Count and Noncount: *a/an/some* 28
some/any 29
Is there any . . .?/Are there any . . .? ... 30
The Paragraph: The Topic Sentence 32

UNIT **4** Your Health 35
should 36
because 37
Reflexive Pronouns 39
Detail Sentences: Actions 40
REVIEW: UNITS 3 AND 4 43

UNIT **5** Animals of the World 45
Superlative Adjectives: *-est* 46
Comparative and
Superlative Adjectives 47
Why Questions 48
Detail Sentences: Animals/Things 50

UNIT **6** Then and Now 53
used to 54
didn't use to/never used to 55
Past Progressive Tense 56
Past Progressive + *when* 57
Detail Sentences: People 58
REVIEW: UNITS 5 AND 6 61

UNIT **7** This Year 63
Future: *will* 64
will/won't 66
a/an or *the* 67
Detail Sentences: Places 68

UNIT **8** It's Fun! 71
It's fun to 72
have to/don't have to 73
has to/doesn't have to 74
Conjunction: *so* 75
Writing Sentences: *and, but, so* 76
REVIEW: UNITS 7 AND 8 79

UNIT **9** My Abilities 81
could/couldn't 82
Comparisons: *good/bad* 83
Subject and Object Pronouns 84
Writing a Postcard 86

UNIT **10** I Want to Be a Star! 89
want + to be/to do 90
What do you want to do? 92
It's + adjective + *to* + verb 93
Comparative Adjectives: *more* 94
Superlative Adjectives: *the most* 95
The Paragraph: Write About Yourself .. 96
REVIEW: UNITS 9 AND 10 99

Antonyms 101
Prefixes 102
Suffixes 103
The Senses 104
Word List 105

Ordinal Numbers

1st 2nd 3rd 4th 5th

Jon is the first person in line.
Jon's brother is the second person in line.
Jon's sister is the third person in line.
Kate is the fourth person in line.
Meg is the fifth person in line.

1st	first	
2nd	second	
3rd	third	
4th	fourth	
5th	fifth	
6th	sixth	
7th	seventh	
8th	eighth	
9th	ninth	
10th	tenth	

Prepositions of Time: *in, on, at*

Jon's birthday is in May.
His birthday is on May 8th.
Jon's birthday party is on Saturday, May 12th.
Jon's party is in the afternoon.
His party is at two o'clock.

Past Tense: *was*

Yesterday

Was it cold and windy yesterday?
Yes, it was.

Last Sunday

Was it rainy and cloudy last Sunday?
No, it wasn't.

Past Tense: Regular Verbs

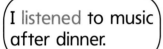

Regular verbs end in *-ed.*

listen → listened   touch → touched
look → looked   walk → walked
play → played   wash → washed
smell → smelled   watch → watched
taste → tasted

Past Tense: Irregular Verbs

Irregular verbs don't end in *-ed.*

drink → drank	read → read
eat → ate	run → ran
get → got	see → saw
go → went	

She drank some water after she played tennis.

They went to the movies last weekend.

MOVIE

Did you eat any candy yesterday?

Yes, I ate two pieces.

Quantities

a piece of cake

a bowl of rice

a can of soup

a cup of tea

a slice of pizza

a glass of milk

a jar of jam

a bottle of water

a bunch of grapes

a bag of potatoes

a box of cereal

a container of juice

a loaf of bread

a stick of butter

Hello!

All About Us

Meg is tall.

Meg is taller than Jon.

Mike is young.

Mike is younger than Jon.

Kate's hair is short.

Kate's hair is shorter than Meg's hair.

Kate's grandfather is old.

Kate's grandfather is older than Kate's grandmother.

Jon's hands are big.

Jon's hands are bigger than Mike's hands.

Kate's legs are long.

Kate's legs are longer than Meg's legs.

Adjectives

> **Adjectives can come after the verb _be_. Use _and_ with more than one adjective after the verb _be_.**
>
> Meg's hair is curly.
> Meg's hair is curly and blond.
>
> **Adjectives can come before a noun. Do not use _and_ with more than one adjective before a noun.**
>
> Meg has curly hair.
> Meg has curly blond hair.

A. Change the sentences. Write the adjectives after the verb _be_.

1. Kate has a nice red bike.

Kate's bike is nice and red.

2. Jon has a big sunny room.

_____

3. Mr. Long has a shiny blue car.

_____

4. Kate has a juicy red apple.

_____

B. Write sentences with _has_. Put the adjectives before the noun.

1. Jon's hair is straight and dark.

Jon has straight dark hair.

2. Kate's hair is short and black.

_____

3. Kate's skirt is long and yellow.

_____

4. Meg's kitten is small and soft.

_____

Comparative Adjectives: *-er*

> **Comparative adjectives show how two things are different. To compare two things, add *-er* to the adjective and use *than*.**
>
> Meg is taller than Jon.

A. Complete the sentences.

1. Meg is _____ younger than _____ Kate. (young)

2. Jon's hair is _____ Mike's hair. (dark)

3. Meg's bike is _____ Jon's bike. (new)

4. Jon is _____ Kate. (short)

5. Mike's hair is _____ Jon's hair. (light)

6. Jon is _____ Meg. (old)

7. Kate's legs are _____ Meg's legs. (long)

8. Kate's cat is _____ Meg's cat. (young)

9. My desk is _____ your desk. (small)

10. Today is _____ yesterday. (cold)

Yesterday

Today

B. Talk to two people in your class. Answer the questions about them.

Example:

Who is shorter?

<u>Jon is shorter than Kate.</u>

1. Who is older?

_____

2. Who has longer hair?

_____

3. Who is taller?

_____

4. Who is younger?

_____

5. Whose hands are bigger?

_____

6. Whose feet are smaller?

_____

7. Whose hair is darker?

_____

8. Whose arms are longer?

_____

Time Clause: *when*

When do you get scared?

I get scared *when I see spiders*.

Complete the sentences. Use *when.*

I see a scary movie   my sister takes my toys
I stay up very late   we win the soccer game
I have a test

1. I get angry *when my sister takes my toys.* _____

2. I get excited _____ _____

3. I get tired _____ _____

4. I get nervous _____ _____

5. I get scared _____ _____

Writing Sentences: *and, but*

> **You can connect sentences with the conjunctions** *and* **and** *but*.
>
> **Use** *and* **to show ideas are similar.**
>
> Meg washes the dishes on Saturday morning.
> Meg cleans her room on Saturday morning.
> Meg washes the dishes *and* she cleans her room on Saturday morning.
>
> **Use** *but* **to show ideas are different.**
>
> Jon doesn't sleep late on Saturday.
> Jon sleeps late on Sunday.
> Jon doesn't sleep late on Saturday *but* he sleeps late on Sunday.

Write one sentence. Use *and* **or** *but*.

1. Meg can play tennis. She can swim.

   Meg can play tennis and she can swim.

2. Mike washed the dishes. He cleaned his room.

   _____

3. Jon likes to watch movies. He doesn't like scary movies.

   _____

4. Meg went to the zoo. She saw the lions.

   _____

5. Mike wants to read a book. The radio is too loud.

   _____

6. Mike has some cake. He doesn't have any milk.

   _____

Who is taller
Who is taller
Kate or Meg?
Kate or Meg?

Don't you know?
Can't you see?
Kate is taller than Meg!

Who is younger
Who is younger
Mike or Jon?
Mike or Jon?

Don't you know?
Can't you see?
Mike is younger than Jon!

Meg is taller than Mike.

Talk about the pictures.

bigger   longer   older   shorter   smaller   younger

Last Weekend

Meg studied before she watched TV.

Mike went to sleep after he took a shower.

Jon rode his bike before he went to school.

Kate made cookies after she ate dinner.

Past Tense: Regular Verbs

> **Regular verbs end in -ed in the past tense. Don't use -ed in negative sentences.**
>
> Last night, Jon watched TV. He didn't watch cartoons.
>
> | | | |
> |---|---|---|
> | call → **called** | study → **studied** | |
> | close → **closed** | talk → **talked** | |
> | cry → **cried** | visit → **visited** | |
> | listen → **listened** | walk → **walked** | |
> | look → **looked** | watch → **watched** | |
> | smell → **smelled** | | |
>
> close + d = **closed**
> study + d = **studied**

A. Complete the sentences.

1. They _____ smelled _____ the cookies in the oven. (smell)

2. Yesterday Kate _____ in the park with her grandmother. (walk)

3. Mike _____ with his friends on the telephone. (talk)

4. Last night Jon _____ to music after dinner. (listen)

B. Complete the sentences. Use *didn't*.

1. Yesterday Jon watched TV. He _____ didn't listen _____ to music. (listen)

2. Last night it was hot. Meg _____ the window. (close)

3. Kate and Mike _____ at the kitchen table. (study)

4. Meg smelled the flower, but she

   _____ at it. (look)

Past Tense: Irregular Verbs

> **Irregular verbs don't end in -ed in the past tense. Don't use irregular past tense forms in negative sentences.**
>
> We ate hamburgers for lunch yesterday.
> We didn't eat any vegetables.
>
> | | | | |
> |---|---|---|---|
> | buy → **bought** | go → **went** | ride → **rode** | swim → **swam** |
> | do → **did** | hear → **heard** | run → **ran** | take → **took** |
> | drink → **drank** | make → **made** | see → **saw** | wear → **wore** |
> | eat → **ate** | meet → **met** | sing → **sang** | write → **wrote** |
> | get → **got** | read → **read** | sleep → **slept** | |

A. Complete the sentences.

1. Last night we _____ *sang* _____ songs. (sing)

2. Kate _____ her friend at the movies yesterday. (meet)

3. Meg _____ in her friend's pool. (swim)

4. He _____ a big glass of milk. (drink)

B. Complete the sentences. Use *didn't*.

1. Jon _____ to school. (walk)

2. She _____ her new dress to the party. (wear)

3. They _____ hamburgers for dinner. (make)

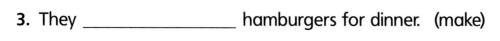

C. What did you do last weekend? Talk with a partner.

 read a book

 wash the dishes

 ride a bike

 play baseball

 study

 eat lunch

 talk on the telephone

 watch TV

 go to the movies

? your own idea

D. Write sentences about the things you did and didn't do.

1. Last weekend I _____.

2. Yesterday I didn't _____.

3. _____

4. _____

5. _____

6. _____

7. _____

8. _____

before/after

Use _before_ and _after_ to tell when something happened.

Jon watched TV _before_ he ate dinner.

A

B

Kate drank water _after_ she played tennis.

A

B

Look at the pictures. Write _before_ or _after_.

1. A  B

Jon listened to music _____ he did his homework.

2. A  B

Kate looked out the window _____ she went outside.

3. A  B

Mike brushed his teeth _____ he went to sleep.

4. A  B

Kate walked in the park _____ she went shopping.

Writing Sentences: *or*

Use the conjunction *or* to combine sentences. Use *or* to show a choice between two ideas. Change the subject in the second sentence to a pronoun *(he, she, they).*

Jon can walk to school. Jon can ride his bike to school.
subject   subject

Jon can walk to school or he can ride his bike to school.
       pronoun

A. Write one sentence. Use *or.* Change the subject in the second sentence to a pronoun.

1. Meg can watch TV. Meg can listen to the radio.

   _____

2. I can make cookies. I can buy cookies at the store.

   _____

3. Jon can play tennis. Jon can go to the zoo.

   _____

4. Kate can read a book. Kate can play outside.

   _____

5. You can have chicken for dinner. You can have hamburgers.

   _____

B. Write a sentence with *or.*

Next weekend I can _____.

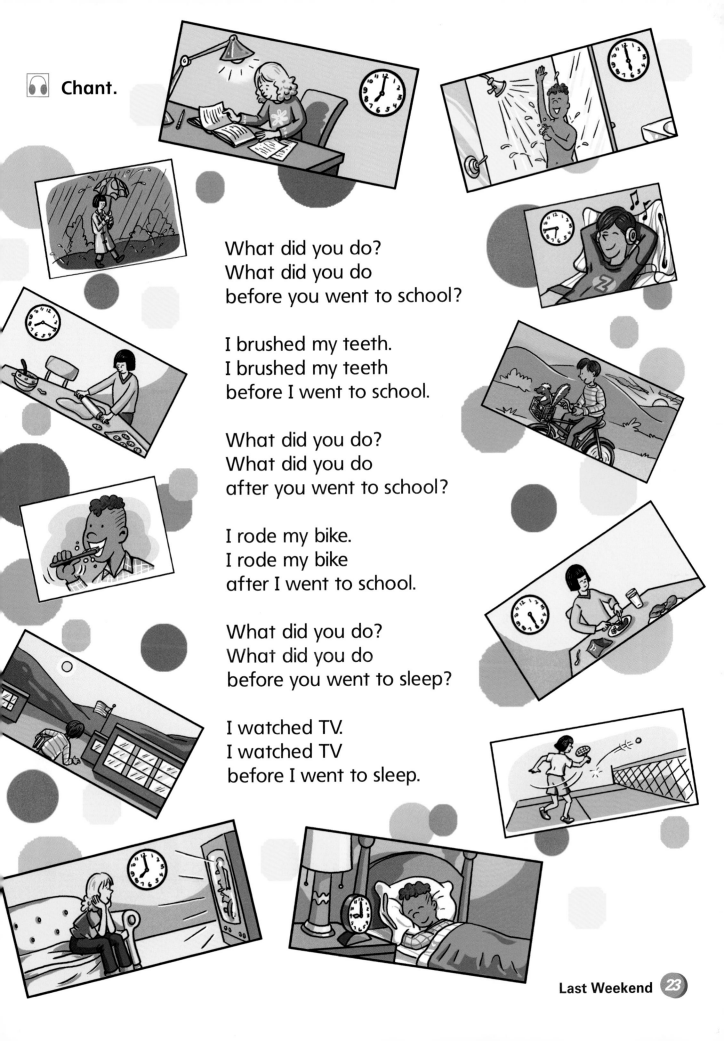

What did you do?
What did you do
before you went to school?

I brushed my teeth.
I brushed my teeth
before I went to school.

What did you do?
What did you do
after you went to school?

I rode my bike.
I rode my bike
after I went to school.

What did you do?
What did you do
before you went to sleep?

I watched TV.
I watched TV
before I went to sleep.

Kate read a book before she washed the dishes.
Kate washed the dishes after she read a book.

Work with a partner. Talk about the pictures.

Review: Units 1 and 2

Vocabulary
Unit 1

🎧 **Listen and check.**

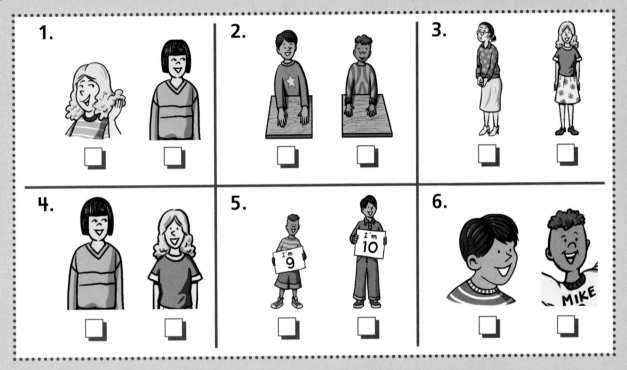

Unit 2

🎧 **A. Listen. Find the picture. Write the number.**

🎧 **B. Listen again. Write the sentences on a piece of paper.**

Review: Units 1 and 2

Grammar
Unit 1

A. | Adjectives | **Write sentences.**

1. hair / short / Kate / black / has

_____

2. dog / Mike's / and / black / is / big

_____

B. | Comparative Adjectives | **Complete the sentences.**

1. Kate is _____ Meg. (tall)

2. My bike is _____ Mike's bike. (new)

3. His kitten is _____ Meg's kitten. (small)

4. Kate's hair is _____ Meg's hair. (short)

5. Kate is _____ Meg. (older)

Unit 2

| Past Tense: Regular and Irregular Verbs | **Write the past tense.**

1. study   _____
2. talk   _____
3. go   _____
4. listen   _____
5. eat   _____

6. wash   _____
7. drink   _____
8. cry   _____
9. ride   _____
10. swim   _____

Let's Eat!

There's some milk in the refrigerator.

There isn't any cereal in the cabinet.

There are some tomatoes on the shelf.

There is = There's

There aren't any apples in the refrigerator.

Count and Noncount: *a/an/some*

Some nouns can be counted. They can be singular or plural.	Some nouns cannot be counted. They do not have a plural form.

Some nouns can be counted. They can be singular or plural.

singular	plural
banana	bananas
carrot	carrots
grape	grapes
strawberry	strawberries
tomato	tomatoes
apple	apples
orange	oranges

Some nouns cannot be counted. They do not have a plural form.

bread
cereal
juice
milk
rice
sugar
toast
water

Use *a* or *an* with singular count nouns.

There's a carrot on the table.
There's an apple in the refrigerator.

Use *some* with noncount nouns and plural count nouns.

There are some bananas on the table.
There's some juice in the refrigerator.

Complete the sentences. Use *a, an,* or *some.*

1. There's _____ cereal on the shelf.

2. Meg ate _____ apple after school.

3. I'm going to eat _____ banana before I go to the park.

4. Jon wants _____ carrots for lunch.

5. Kate and Meg made _____ bread yesterday.

6. Yesterday Kate's rabbit ate _____ carrot.

7. Mike is going to buy _____ orange and _____ strawberries at the supermarket.

some / any

Use *some* in affirmative sentences. Use *any* in negative sentences.

There's some **cereal** in the cabinet.
There isn't any **cereal** on the shelf.

There are some **plates** in the sink.
There aren't any **plates** on the shelf.

Look at the pictures. Complete the sentences.

1. There's some _____ juice in the refrigerator.

2. There isn't any _____ juice in the refrigerator.

3. There are _____ peaches in the basket.

4. There aren't _____ peaches in the basket.

5. There's _____ rice in the bowl.

6. _____ rice in the bowl.

7. _____ cookies in the jar.

8. _____ cookies in the jar.

Is there any...? / Are there any...?

Use *any* with questions.

Is there any **sugar**?

Are there any **grapes**?

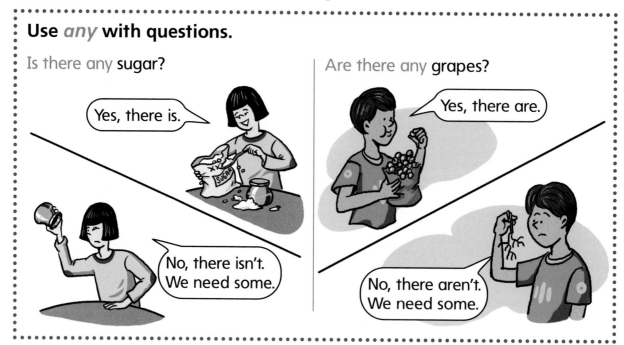

Yes, there is.

No, there isn't.
We need some.

Yes, there are.

No, there aren't.
We need some.

A. Write the questions.

1. _Is there any_____ milk in the refrigerator? Yes, there is.

2. _____ oranges? Yes, there are.

3. _____ bread? No, there isn't. We need some.

4. _____ apples? No, there aren't. We need some.

5. _____ rice in the cabinet? Yes, there is.

6. _____ tomatoes? No, there aren't. We need some.

B. Look at the picture. Write questions and answers. Use *Is there any . . . ?* or *Are there any . . . ?*

1. Are there any oranges?

   Yes, there are.

2.

3.

4.

5.

6.

7.

The Paragraph: The Topic Sentence

The topic sentence tells the main idea of a paragraph. It is usually the first sentence in the paragraph. Indent the topic sentence.

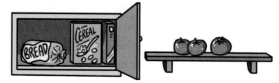

Healthy Foods

indent

There are many healthy foods in our house. There's some milk in our refrigerator. There's some cereal in the cabinet. There are some tomatoes on the kitchen shelf, but there aren't any bananas. We are going to buy some today.

Use the pictures and the sentences to write a paragraph. Begin with the topic sentence.

They ate some strawberries in the park.
Jon and Meg went to the park on Sunday.
Jon rode his bike.
Meg picked some flowers.

1.

_____

_____

_____

Mike got scared.
There were some scary animals.
Kate and Mike went to the zoo.
Kate talked to the tigers.

2.

_____

_____

_____

Are there any carrots?
Yes, there are. Yes, there are.
Are there any carrots?
There are some on the shelf.

Are there any oranges?
No, there aren't. No, there aren't.
Are there any tomatoes?
You can see for yourself.

Are there any bananas?
Yes, there are. Yes, there are.
Are there any bananas?
There are some on the shelf.

Are there any strawberries?
No, there aren't. No, there aren't.
Are there any cookies?
You can see for yourself!

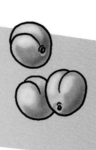

Are there any peaches?
No, there aren't. Yes, there are.

Is there any milk?
Yes, there is. No, there isn't.

Work with a partner. Ask and answer questions about the pictures.

Picture A

Picture B

Your Health

should

I have a headache.

You should go to bed.

He has a sore throat.
She has a stomachache.
They are hungry.

He should take some medicine.
She should drink some tea.
They should eat.

Give advice. Write sentences with *should*.

1. I'm tired.

You should go to sleep early.

2. Kate has a toothache.

_____

3. Mike and Jon are hungry.

_____

4. My sister hurt her leg.

_____

5. I feel sick.

_____

6. Meg's mother has a stomachache.

_____

7. Jon has a cold.

_____

because

> **Combine sentences with *because* to show *why*.**
>
> The movie was sad. Meg cried.
> Meg cried because the movie was sad.

A. Combine the sentences. Use *because*.

1. It was raining. We went home.

   _____

2. It was delicious. I ate two pieces of cake.

   _____

3. I stayed up very late. I'm tired.

   _____

4. The music is too loud. I can't study.

   _____

5. I was sick. I took medicine.

   _____

6. I ate too many cookies. I have a stomachache.

   _____

B. Match and write sentences with *because*.

we have our umbrellas	he played tennis
she wants to eat	they are pretty
I like the flowers	it's too small
he's very tired	it's raining
I can't wear this shirt	she's hungry

1. We have our umbrellas because it's raining.

2. _____

3. _____

4. _____

5. _____

C. Look at the pictures. Complete the sentences. Use *because*.

1.

Jon should drink some tea _____.

2.

Meg should go to sleep early _____.

3.

Mike should take some medicine _____.

Reflexive Pronouns

I can eat a big pizza by myself.

He made a picture by himself.

Can she ride a bike by herself?

Wash the dishes by yourself!

A. Match. Draw a line.

1. I
2. you
3. he
4. she

myself   herself

himself   yourself

B. Write sentences.

1. herself / by / is making a sandwich / she

_____

2. I / myself / by / am drawing a picture

_____

3. can do the puzzle / by / he / himself

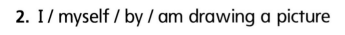

_____

4. by / study / you / yourself / can

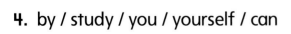

_____

Detail Sentences: Describe Actions

Detail sentences **help describe actions. They give more information about the main idea of the paragraph.**

Topic Sentence: You should exercise and eat healthy food every day.

Detail Sentences:
You can ride your bike or you can play sports.
Drink four glasses of water every day because water is good for you.
Eat green vegetables and lots of fruit.
Go to bed early and get a lot of rest.

A. Look at the picture. Read the topic sentence.

Topic Sentence: Meg should stay home today because she feels sick.

B. Check the detail sentences that give more information about the topic sentence in Exercise A.

☐ She ate too much candy yesterday.   ☐ Meg is tall and she has blond hair.

☐ She is excited.   ☐ She is younger than Kate.

☐ Her stomach hurts.   ☐ She can play outdoors.

C. Use the topic and detail sentences to write a paragraph about Meg. Begin with the topic sentence. Indent the topic sentence.

🎧 **Chant.**

I feel sick.
What should I do?
You should go to bed.
That's what's best for you!

I have a toothache.
What should I do?
You should go to the dentist.
That's the best thing to do.

I hurt my arm.
What should I do?
You should go to the doctor.
That's what's best for you!

I'm so tired!
What should I do?
You should go to sleep early.
That's the best thing to do.

I have a headache.
I feel sick.

Look at the pictures. Complete the sentences with words from the box. Then complete the puzzle.

toothache	hungry	sore throat	tired
headache	cold	sick	

Across

1. I feel sick.

3. I'm ______________.

4. I have a ______________.

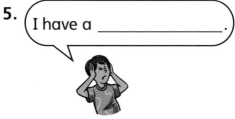

5. I have a ______________.

Down

2. I have a ______________.

3. I have a ______________.

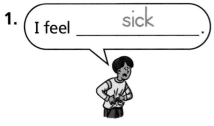

6. I'm ______________.

Review: Units 3 and 4

Vocabulary
Unit 3

🎧 Listen and check.

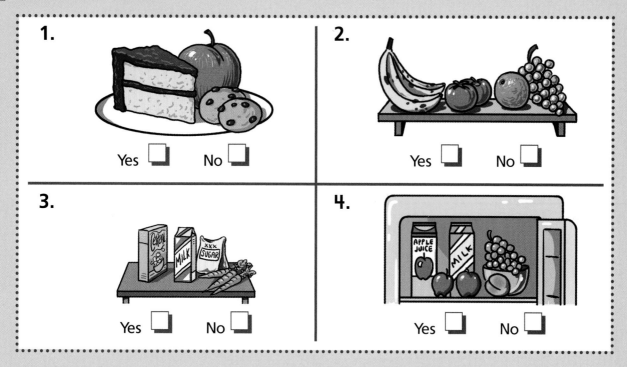

1.
Yes ☐ No ☐

2.
Yes ☐ No ☐

3.
Yes ☐ No ☐

4.
Yes ☐ No ☐

Unit 4

🎧 A. Listen. Find the picture. Write the number.

🎧 B. Listen again. Write the sentences on a piece of paper.

Review: Units 3 and 4

Grammar
Unit 3

| Is there any . . . ? Are there any . . . ? | **Look at the pictures. Complete the questions. Write the answers.** |

1. _____ soup in the bowl? _____

2. _____ peaches in the basket? _____

3. _____ bread on the shelf? _____

4. _____ milk on the table? _____

5. _____ cookies in the jar? _____

6. _____ cereal in the cabinet? _____

Unit 4

A. | because | **Write sentences.**

1. It was raining. We didn't play tennis.

_____

2. The music is too loud. She can't do her homework.

_____

B. | myself, yourself, himself, herself | **Complete the sentences.**

1. Kate is eleven years old. She can walk to school by _____ .

2. He is six years old. He can ride a bike by _____ .

3. I love to do puzzles by _____ .

4. Can you make a cake by _____ ?

Animals of the World

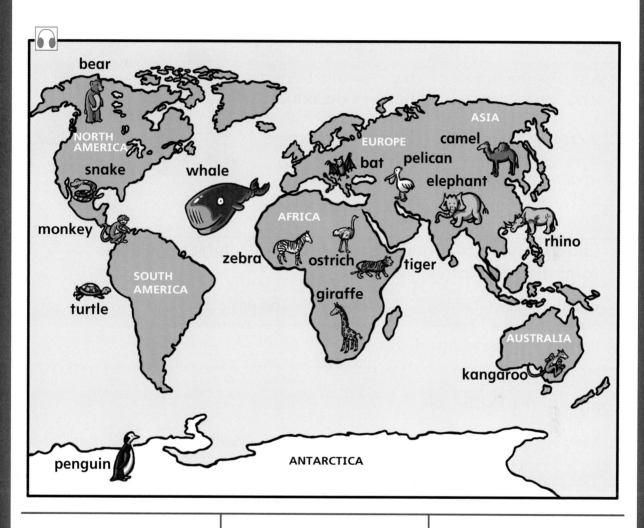

bear

NORTH AMERICA

snake

whale

monkey

turtle

SOUTH AMERICA

ASIA

EUROPE

camel

bat

pelican

elephant

AFRICA

zebra

ostrich

tiger

giraffe

rhino

AUSTRALIA

kangaroo

penguin

ANTARCTICA

monkey

kangaroo

elephant

The kangaroo is bigger than the monkey.
The elephant is bigger than the kangaroo.
The elephant is the biggest.

Superlative Adjectives: -est

Superlative adjectives compare more than two things. Add _the_ and -est to one-syllable adjectives to form the superlative.

Alex is short. Alex is shorter than Tim.
Bob is shorter than Alex.
Bob is the shortest boy on the basketball team.

fast	→ the fastest	big	→ the biggest
long	→ the longest	hot	→ the hottest

short	→ the shortest	large	→ the largest
slow	→ the slowest	nice	→ the nicest
small	→ the smallest		
soft	→ the softest		
tall	→ the tallest		

Change the -y to -i and add -est to two-syllable adjectives to form the superlative.

funny	→ the funniest	pretty	→ the prettiest
happy	→ the happiest	snowy	→ the snowiest
healthy	→ the healthiest		

Complete the sentences.

1. Meg is _____the tallest_____ girl in our class. (tall)

2. The cheetah is _____ animal in the world. (fast)

3. Mike is _____ person in his family. (healthy)

4. Kate is _____ girl in her class. (pretty)

5. Today is _____ day of the summer. (hot)

6. My sister has _____ feet in our family. (small)

Comparative and Superlative Adjectives

adjective	comparative	superlative
big	bigger	the biggest
fast	faster	the fastest
long	longer	the longest
short	shorter	the shortest
slow	slower	the slowest
small	smaller	the smallest
tall	taller	the tallest

A. Complete the sentences.

long

zebra

ostrich

giraffe

The ostrich's neck is longer than the zebra's neck.

The giraffe's neck is _____ the ostrich's neck.

The giraffe has _____ neck.

short

rhino

camel

tiger

The camel's tail is shorter than the tiger's tail.

The rhino's tail is _____ the camel's tail.

The rhino has _____ tail.

B. Talk about all the animals on page 45.

Why Questions

> **Answer *why* questions with *because*.**
>
> Why did you eat three hamburgers?
>
> I ate three hamburgers because I was hungry.

A. Complete the sentences.

1.

Why did you get up early yesterday?

I got up early _____

2.

 _____ a cake?

I made a cake _____

3.

 _____ late?

I slept late _____

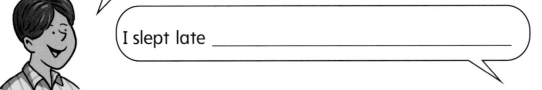

B. Look at the pictures. Write the answers.

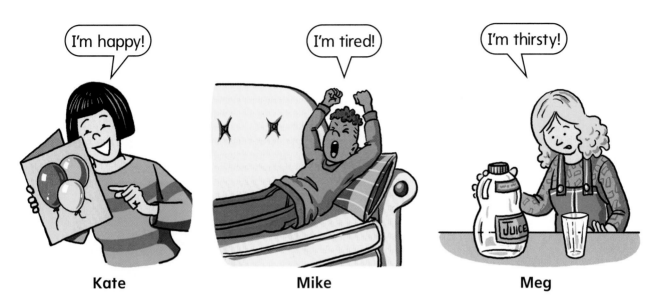

Kate — I'm happy!

Mike — I'm tired!

Meg — I'm thirsty!

1. **Mike:** Why are you happy?

   Kate: _____

2. **Kate:** Why are you tired?

   Mike: _____

3. **Mike:** Why are you thirsty?

   Meg: _____

C. Why are *you* happy? Write the answer. Draw.

_____

Detail Sentences: Describe Animals and Things

> **Detail sentences help describe animals and things.**
>
> ### My Favorite Animal
>
> topic sentence
>
> Dusty is my favorite animal. She is a dark gray cat. She loves to play. She loves to run, but she's slow. She's slower than my friend's cat. She is the slowest cat on our street. I like her because she has the shortest tail. She is very funny.
>
>

A. Draw a picture of your favorite animal.

B. Write a paragraph. Use detail sentences.

My Favorite Animal

_____ is my favorite animal. _____

_____

_____

_____

🎧 **Chant.**

Slowest—Fastest
Biggest—Smallest

Slow—Fast—Small

Longest—Shortest
Largest—Tallest

Long—Short—Tall

Who is the shortest?
I'm the shortest!

Who is the biggest?
I'm the biggest!

Who is the tallest?
I'm the tallest!
I'm the tallest of all!

The elephant is bigger than the bat.
The giraffe has the longest neck.

Work with a partner. Find and color the animals. Talk about them.

bat	monkey	elephant	turtle	ostrich
rhino	kangaroo	giraffe	tiger	alligator

Then and Now

Many years ago . . .

People used to sew by hand.

Now they use electric sewing machines.

People used to read and write by candlelight.

Now they use electric lights.

People used to travel by horse and buggy.

Now they travel by plane and by car.

People used to wash clothes by hand.

Now they use washing machines and dryers.

used to

I used to collect dolls.

Now I collect stamps.

A. Write sentences with *used to*.

1. (New York) I used to live in New York. Now I live in Korea.

2. (bike) _____ Now I ride a motorcycle.

3. (tennis) _____ Now I play baseball.

4. (animals) _____ Now I draw flowers.

5. (candy) _____ Now I eat healthy food.

6. (dog) _____ Now I have a parrot.

B. Complete the sentences. Draw.

I used to _____.

Now I _____.

didn't use to/never used to

Use *didn't use to* or *never used to* to talk about something that wasn't true in the past but is true now.

Last Year	Today

They didn't use to like broccoli, but they do now!
They never used to eat broccoli, but now they love it!

A. What didn't you use to do? Tell a friend. Add to the list.

play the piano
eat candy
go to the movies
make my bed
dance
ice-skate

stay up late
drink soda

_____
_____
_____
_____

B. Write sentences about yourself.

1. I never used to play the piano, but now I play every day.

2. _____

3. _____

4. _____

5. _____

6. _____

7. _____

Past Progressive Tense

> **Use the past progressive tense to describe a continuous action in the past.**
>
> What were the children doing at ten o'clock last night?
> They were sleeping.
>
> What was Meg doing before dinner?
> She was playing the piano.

What were the people doing at 7:30 in the morning? Write sentences.

eating breakfast	brushing her teeth	making the bed
getting dressed	cleaning the house	sweeping the floor
feeding the dog	waking up	

1. Meg was getting dressed. _____

2. _____

3. _____

4. _____

5. _____

6. _____

Past Progressive + *when*

> **Use *when* to show that one continuous action in the past was interrupted by another action.**
>
> Jon was reading when the phone rang.
> Meg was washing the dishes when the phone rang.
> Kate was watching TV when the phone rang.

Look at the pictures. Complete the sentences.

Meg was eating lunch	Jon was doing his homework
Kate was reading a book	The children were playing at the beach

1. _____

   when it got very windy.

2. _____

   when he heard a loud noise.

3. _____

   when the door bell rang.

4. _____

   when the picture fell down.

Detail Sentences: Describe People

> Detail sentences help describe a person.
>
> When writing about a person
> - tell what the person looks like
> - tell what the person likes and doesn't like
> - tell interesting things about the person
>
> ### My Friend Pam
>
>
>
> **topic sentence**
>
> Pam is my best friend. She has curly red hair and blue eyes. She is tall. She likes to play sports. She used to play soccer every day, but now she plays tennis. Pam loves animals. She used to have three big white cats, but now she has one small white cat.

Write about your friend. Start with a topic sentence.

What does your friend look like?

Does your friend like to . . . ?

read	play tennis	swim	play soccer
ride a bike	sing	go to the zoo	make cookies
go to the movies	sleep late	run	take a walk

My Friend _____

_____

_____

_____

_____

I never used to play the piano.
Play the piano
Play the piano
I never used to play the piano.
Now I play it every day.

I never used to make my bed.
Make my bed
Make my bed
I never used to make my bed.
Now I make it every day.

I never used to eat green vegetables.
Eat green vegetables
Eat green vegetables
I never used to eat green vegetables.
Now I eat them every day.

I never used to stay up late.
Stay up late
Stay up late
Now I always stay up late.
And I'm tired every day!

What was Kate doing last night?
What were the children doing last Saturday?

Work with a partner. Look at the pictures. Ask and answer questions.

Review: Units 5 and 6

Vocabulary

Unit 5

🎧 **Listen and check.**

1. Yes, he is. ☐   No, he isn't. ☐

2. Yes, it does. ☐   No, it doesn't. ☐

3. Yes, it does. ☐   No, it doesn't. ☐

4. Yes, it does. ☐   No, it doesn't. ☐

Unit 6

🎧 **A. Listen and check.**

1. ☐   ☐   2. ☐   ☐

3. ☐   ☐   4. ☐   ☐

🎧 **B. Listen again. Write the sentences on a piece of paper.**

Review: Units 5 and 6

Grammar

Unit 5

| *Why* questions | **Write the questions.**

1. _____

I went to sleep early because I was tired.

2. _____

She ate three pieces of pizza because she was hungry.

3. _____

He went to the beach because he likes to swim.

4. _____

They made a cake because it was their father's birthday.

Unit 6

| Past Progressive | **Look at the pictures. Complete the sentences.**

1. _____

when the phone rang.

2. _____

when the phone rang.

3. _____

when the phone rang.

4. _____

when the phone rang.

This Year

Future: *will*

Use *will* to ask and talk about the future.

When will Meg have her party?
She'll have her party on June 7th.

When will Jon go to the soccer game?
He'll go to the soccer game next Tuesday.

When will Kate and Meg go to the circus?
They'll go to the circus this weekend.

| he'll = he will | she'll = she will |
| I'll = I will | they'll = they will |

JUNE						
SUN	MON	TUE	WED	THU	FRI	SAT
	1 TODAY	2 SOCCER GAME	3	4	5	6 CIRCUS
7 MEG'S PARTY	8	9	10	11	12	13 MOVIES
14 VISIT GRANDMA	15	16	17	18	19	20
21	22	23	24	25	26	27
28	29	30				

A. Write questions. Use *will*.

1. (you) <u>When will you visit your grandmother?</u>
   I'll visit my grandmother next weekend.

2. (Meg and Mike) _____
   They'll go to the movies next Saturday at 3:00.

3. (Jon) _____
   He'll do his homework before dinner.

4. (Kate) _____
   She'll go shopping with her mother tomorrow.

B. Look at the pictures. Write answers. Use *he'll, she'll,* or *they'll*.

1. When will Meg go to the movies?

_____

2. When will Jon have his birthday party?

_____

3. When will Kate and her sister visit their grandfather?

_____

C. What are your chores? Draw yourself doing a chore. Show the time.

_____

will / won't

Use **will** and **won't** to make promises about the future.

> I'll take out the garbage every day.

> I won't ride my bike in the street.

won't = will not

A. Look at the chart. Check.

This Year

I will	I won't	
✓		clean my room every day
		bother my sister or brother
		watch TV at night
		share my games or books
		eat candy
		be kind to animals
		go swimming by myself
		ride my bike in the street
		do my homework every day

B. Write sentences. Use **will** or **won't**.

1. I'll clean my room every day. _____

2. _____

3. _____

4. _____

a/an or the

> Use *a/an* + a noun the <u>first time</u> you talk about the noun.
> Use *the* + a noun when you talk about the noun <u>again</u>.
>
> Meg has a book. The book is about birds. She loves the book.
>
> Yesterday Jon bought an umbrella.
> He opened the umbrella. The umbrella was broken.
>
> **Note: Use *an* before a word that begins with a vowel sound.**

Complete the sentences with *a*, *an*, or *the*.

1. Meg has _____ new bike. _____ bike is

   bright red. Meg rides _____ bike to school

   every day.

2. Jon is having _____ birthday party.

   _____ party is this Sunday. Will you come

   to _____ party?

3. Meg had _____ apple. She ate _____ apple for lunch.

   _____ apple was very juicy.

4. The Smiths live in _____ old house. _____ house

   is 120 years old. Sometimes they get scared

   in _____ house, but they won't move. They

   love _____ house.

5. Mike has _____ big brown dog. He loves to

   pet _____ dog. _____ dog loves it.

   _____ dog is Mike's favorite animal.

Detail Sentences: Describe Places

Detail sentences help describe a place.

When writing about a place:
- **tell what the place looks like**

    The beach has many shells and rocks.

- **tell about what you will do there**

    We'll swim every day.

- **tell what you like and don't like about the place**

    There are seagulls flying everywhere.

Sandy Beach

My favorite place is Sandy Beach. My family goes there every year. We always have fun. The beach has many shells and rocks. The sand is white and soft. There are many tall palm trees. There are seagulls flying everywhere. The water is always warm, and it feels very good. This year we'll swim every day and sit under the palm trees.

Write about your favorite place. Write a title. Begin with a topic sentence.

_____

_____

_____

_____

_____

_____

This year . . .
　I'll share my books and games.
　I'll put my clothes away.
　I'll take out all the garbage.
　I'll clean my room . . . every day!

　I won't eat too much candy!
　I won't bother my little brother!
　I won't forget my chores.
　I'll listen to my mother!

　I'll go to bed really early.
　I won't watch TV at night.
　And when my eyes begin to close,
　I'll turn out all the lights!

I'll make my bed every day.
I won't eat too much candy.

Work with a partner. Look at the pictures. Make promises. Use the words in the box.

every day	on Sunday	tomorrow	this weekend

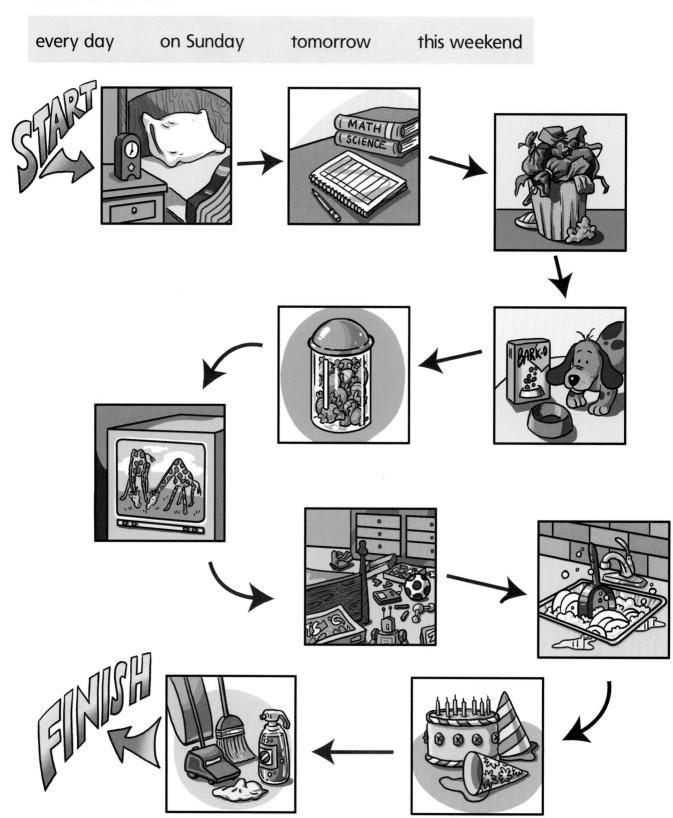

It's Fun!

It's fun to collect stamps.

It's fun to go to the movies.

It's fun to dance.

It's fun to take photographs.

It's fun to plant a garden.

It's fun to go swimming.

It's fun to look for insects.

It's fun to make jewelry.

It's fun to . . .

It's fun to go to the zoo.

It's boring to go shopping.

It's easy to make cookies.

It's difficult to climb a tree.

What do you think? Write sentences.

boring	bake a cake	go to the movies
difficult	clean my room	play the piano
easy	climb a mountain	use a computer
fun		

1. It's boring to clean my room.

2. _____

3. _____

4. _____

5. _____

6. _____

have to/don't have to

A. What do you have to do? Complete the chart. Check.

I have to . . .	I don't have to . . .	
		clean my room
		wash the dishes
		take out the garbage
		get up early
		water the plants
		do my homework
		feed my pet

B. Look at the chart. Write sentences. Use *have to* or *don't have to*.

1. _____

2. _____

3. _____

4. _____

5. _____

6. _____

7. _____

has to / doesn't have to

Jon has to water the plants every morning.

Jon doesn't have to take out the garbage.

A. Work with a partner. Ask *What do you have to do?* Complete the chart. Add more chores your partner *has to* and *doesn't have to* do. Check.

has to . . .	doesn't have to . . .	[Name] _____
		sweep the floor
		wash the dishes
		take out the garbage
		get up early
		water the plants
		do homework
		feed a pet

B. Look at the chart. Write some sentences about your partner. Use *he* or *she* and *has to* or *doesn't have to*.

1. _____

2. _____

3. _____

4. _____

5. _____

6. _____

Conjunction: *so*

Combine sentences with *so* to show the result of something.

Mike was thirsty so
he drank some cold milk.
result

It was raining so
they didn't go outside.
result

A. Write one sentence. Use *so*.

1. Kate was tired. She went to bed early.

Kate was tired so she went to bed early.

2. Jon had a headache. He took some medicine.

_____

3. It was cold outside. The children wore winter coats.

_____

B. Complete the sentences. Use *so* and *he, she,* or *they*.

made a cake	didn't go outside
ate some strawberries	went to the doctor
went to the beach	closed their eyes

1. Meg was hungry so she ate some strawberries_____.

2. It was a beautiful day _____.

3. Jon had a stomachache _____.

4. Mike was very tired _____.

5. The movie was scary _____.

6. Kate didn't have any homework _____.

Writing Sentences: *and, but, so*

Mike can play tennis and he can swim.

Kate can swim but she can't play tennis.

It was cold today so Mike didn't go swimming.

Complete the sentences.

1. Every morning Jon makes his bed _____ he sweeps his floor.
   <small>so / and</small>

2. Meg got up late _____ she got to school late.
   <small>so / but</small>

3. The soup was very hot _____ I ate it very slowly.
   <small>but / so</small>

4. I want to go swimming _____ it's raining today.
   <small>and / but</small>

5. Next Saturday I'm going to the movies _____ my sister is going to the zoo.
   <small>so / and</small>

6. I watered the plants _____ I didn't feed my dog.
   <small>but / and</small>

7. Kate had a sore throat _____ she didn't go to school.
   <small>so / but</small>

8. I eat vegetables _____ I don't like broccoli!
   <small>and / but</small>

🎧 **Chant.**

It's fun!
What's fun?
It's fun to ride a bike!

It's fun!
What's fun?
It's fun to take a hike.

It's fun!
What's fun?
It's fun to sing and play.

It's fun!
What's fun?
It's fun to swim all day!

It's fun to . . . It's easy to . . .

Work with a partner. Talk about the pictures.

boring   easy   fun   difficult

Review: Units 7 and 8

Vocabulary

Unit 7

Listen and check.

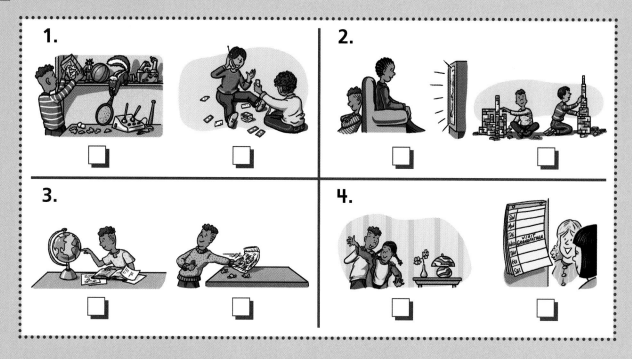

Unit 8

A. Listen. Find the picture. Write the number.

B. Listen again. Write the sentences on a piece of paper.

Review: Units 7 and 8

Grammar
Unit 7

| Future: *will* | **Write questions and answers.** |

1. (Meg and Jon) _____

They'll do their chores after breakfast.

2. (Mike) _____

He'll clean his room on Sunday.

3. When will Mike visit his grandmother?

_____

4. When will you do your homework?

_____

I won't forget to visit my grandmother.

Unit 8

| has to/have to, doesn't have to/don't have to | **Write sentences.** |

	has to/have to	doesn't have to/ don't have to	
1. Meg and Jon	✓		wash the dishes
2. Mike		✓	take out the garbage
3. Kate and Mike		✓	clean their rooms
4. Jon	✓		feed the dog

1. _____

2. _____

3. _____

4. _____

My Abilities

When I was young, . . .

I couldn't tie my shoelaces.

But now I can.

I couldn't catch a ball.

But now I can.

I couldn't climb a tree.

But now I can.

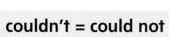

couldn't = could not

could/couldn't

Use *could* and *couldn't* to talk about your abilities when you were young.

When I was three, I could draw.
I couldn't write.

When I was four, I could run fast.
I couldn't ride a bicycle.

play soccer

make my bed

climb a tree

dress myself

tie my shoelaces

wash the dishes

use a computer

ride a horse

Write sentences about yourself. Use *could* or *couldn't*.

1. When I was young, _____

2. _____

3. _____

4. _____

5. _____

Comparisons: *good/bad*

The adjectives *good* and *bad* have irregular comparative and superlative forms.

good—better—the best

Meg is a good runner.

Jon is a better runner than Meg.

Kate is the best runner on our team.

bad—worse—the worst

On Monday the weather was bad.

On Tuesday the weather was worse than on Monday.

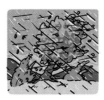

Today is the worst day of the week.

Write the correct form of the adjective.

1. He is _____ student in the class.   (good)

2. I am a _____ dancer.   (good)

3. This is _____ book in the whole library.   (bad)

4. Mike is a _____ dancer than Jon.   (good)

5. Kate is _____ student in her class.   (good)

6. Today the weather is very _____.   (bad)

7. She is _____ tennis player on the team.   (bad)

8. Jon's cold is _____ than my cold.   (bad)

Subject and Object Pronouns

A **subject pronoun** replaces a subject.

Meg likes ice cream.
She likes ice cream.
subject
pronoun

An **object pronoun** replaces an object.

Jon saw a dog in the park.
Jon saw it in the park.
object
pronoun

Jon is talking to Meg.
Jon is talking to her.
object
pronoun

Note: An object pronoun can also come after *to*, *for*, and *with*.

subject pronouns		object pronouns	
I	we	me	us
you	you	you	you
he/she/it	they	him/her/it	them

A. Complete the sentences.

1. She gave _____ a birthday present.
   <u>him / he</u>

2. Kate went to the movies with _____ last night.
   <u>we / us</u>

3. _____ called me at 9:00.
   <u>She / Her</u>

4. Will you read this book to _____?
   <u>I / me</u>

5. I saw _____ at the park.
   <u>she / her</u>

6. _____ didn't make cookies yesterday.
   <u>Them / They</u>

7. Is that present for _____?
   <u>us / we</u>

8. Jon played a game with _____ yesterday.
   <u>them / they</u>

B. Complete the sentences with object pronouns.

1. Is your birthday tomorrow? I'm going to buy a present for _____.

2. I met Meg and Jon at the park. It was fun playing with _____.

3. I'm hungry. Can you buy a hamburger for _____?

4. Mike went to a baseball game with Jon. He had a good time with

_____.

5. Jon is talking to Meg. He likes talking to _____.

6. Meg sat between Kate and Mike at the movies.

She was happy to be with _____.

C. Write sentences.

1. talking / I / you / like / to

I like talking to you.

2. her / a / he / letter / wrote / to

_____

3. movies / to / she / them / went / the / with

_____

4. yesterday / me / they / called

_____

5. them / apple pie / for / made / we / an

_____

Writing a Postcard

A postcard has a greeting, a body, a closing, a signature, and an address.

comma

Dear Meg,]— greeting

I had the best vacation! I swam and played tennis every day. I collected rocks and made jewelry. I took photographs of my family. I had fun but it rained the last week. That was the worst week. Did you have a good vacation? Please write to me.]— body

closing —[Your friend,
signature —[Kate
comma

Meg Smith
10 Main Street
Tampa, Florida 33617
USA
]— address

Write a postcard to Meg. Write about your vacation.

When I was young
When I was young
I couldn't ride a bike.

Now I can.
Look at me!
I can ride a bike.

When I was young
When I was young
I couldn't catch a ball.

Now I can.
Look at me!
I can catch a ball.

When I was young
When I was young
I couldn't climb a tree.

Now I can.
Now I can.
Look at me!
Look at me!
Look at me!

Last year Tom couldn't ride a bike. Now he can.

Work with a partner. Look at the pictures. Talk about the children.

Marco   Maria   Lee   Tom   Tina   Jin   Lea

Last Year

Now

I Want to Be a Star!

want + to be

What do you want to be?

When I grow up, I want to be a photographer.

a scientist

a musician

a dancer

a singer

a truck driver

What do you want to be? Check.

I want to be . . .		a musician	
an artist		a photographer	
an astronaut		a scientist	
an athlete		a singer	
a dancer		a truck driver	
a firefighter		a writer	
a movie star	✓		

want + to do

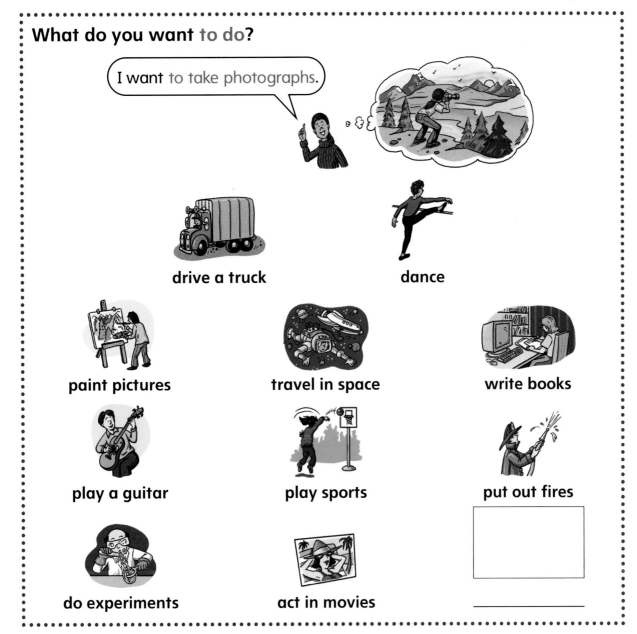

What do you want **to do**?

I want **to take photographs**.

drive a truck   dance

paint pictures   travel in space   write books

play a guitar   play sports   put out fires

do experiments   act in movies   _____

What do you want to do? Check.

I want to . . .				
act in movies	✓	play sports		
dance		put out fires		
do experiments		sing on a stage		
drive a truck		take photographs		
paint pictures		travel in space		
play a guitar		write books		

What do you want to do?

Write what you want to be. Write what you want to do. Draw yourself.

When I grow up, I want to be a movie star. I want to act in movies.

It's + adjective + *to* + verb

It's dangerous to put out fires.

It's exciting to play sports.

It's interesting to do experiments.

It's difficult to write a book.

What do you think? Write some sentences.

dangerous	act in movies	play sports
difficult	dance	put out fires
exciting	do experiments	sing on a stage
interesting	drive a truck	take photographs
	paint pictures	travel in space
	play a guitar	write books

1. It's difficult to play a guitar.

2. _____

3. _____

4. _____

5. _____

6. _____

Comparative Adjectives: *more*

Use *more* with *than* to form the comparative of many long adjectives.

It's more difficult to travel in space than to drive a truck.

Some short adjectives also use *more*.

more fun than
more boring than

Complete the sentences. Use *more . . . than*.

| boring | dangerous | difficult | exciting | fun | interesting |

1. It's more exciting to sing on a stage than _____ to write a book.

2. _____ to play a guitar.

3. _____ to act in a movie.

4. _____ to take photographs.

5. _____ to sing on a stage.

6. _____ to drive a truck.

Superlative Adjectives: *the most*

Use *the most* to form the superlative of many long adjectives.

I want to be an astronaut. It's the most interesting job.

I don't want to be a truck driver. It's the most boring job.

Look at the pictures. Write sentences. Use *the most.*

boring	dangerous	difficult	exciting	interesting

1. I want to be _____.

   It's _____.

2. I don't want to be _____.

   It's _____.

3. I _____.

   _____.

The Paragraph: Write About Yourself

What do you want to be?
What do you want to do?

Use the charts on pages 90 and 91 to write a paragraph about yourself. Use *and* and *because*.

> When I grow up, I want to be an artist. I want to be an artist because I want to paint pictures. It's more fun to be an artist than to be a singer.

_____

_____

_____

_____

_____

_____

_____

Check.

	yes	no
Does your paragraph have a topic sentence?		
Does your paragraph have detail sentences?		
Does your paragraph tell what you want to be?		
Does your paragraph tell what you want to do?		

What do you want to be?
I want to be a star!

What do you want to do?
I want to play the guitar.

What do you want to be?
I want to be a writer.

What do you want to be?
I want to be a firefighter.

What do you want to do?
What do you want to be?

A dancer or a singer—
That's what I want to be!

What does he want to be? He wants to be a dancer.
What does she want to be? She wants to be an artist.

A. Work with a partner. Look at the pictures. Ask about the pictures. Write the words.

a __dancer__

an _____

a _____

an _____

a _____

a _____

a _____

a _____

an _____

B. Find and circle the words from Exercise A.

```
v  c  g  d  a  t  h  l  e  t  e  e  a  q  t
e  d  a  n  c  e  r  m  c  e  y  l  u  p  j
a  r  t  i  s  t  w  r  i  t  e  r  l  f  l
m  u  s  i  c  i  a  n  r  f  d  f  z  q  z
k  j  w  l  f  i  r  e  f  i  g  h  t  e  r
t  s  c  i  e  n  t  i  s  t  z  r  g  b  q
a  s  t  r  o  n  a  u  t  c  h  h  g  k  w
p  h  o  t  o  g  r  a  p  h  e  r  g  f  c
```

Review: Units 9 and 10

Vocabulary

Unit 9

🎧 **Listen and check.**

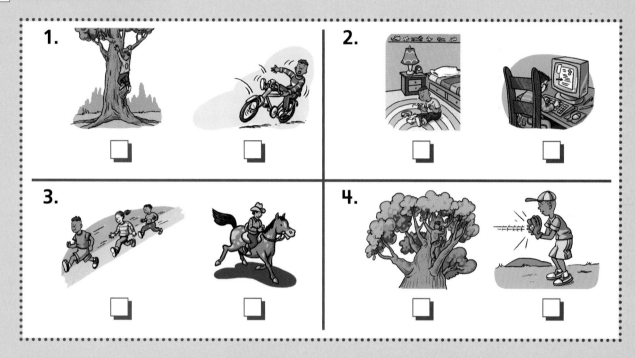

Unit 10

🎧 **A. Listen and check.**

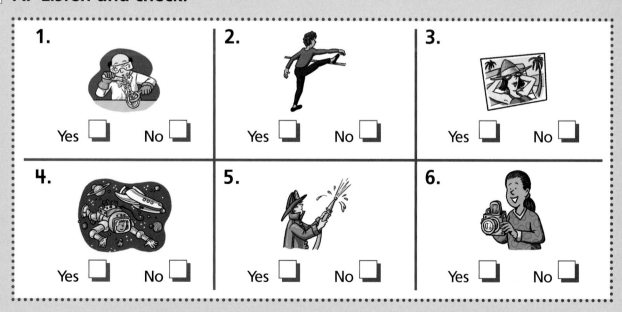

🎧 **B. Listen again. Write the sentences on a piece of paper.**

Review: Units 9 and 10

Grammar

Unit 9

A. | Comparisons: good/bad | **Write the correct form of the adjective.**

1. (good—better—best) Jon is a _____ dancer. He is a _____ dancer than his brother. He is the _____ dancer in his family.

2. (bad—worse—worst) *Star Dogs 2* was a _____ movie. It was the _____ movie on TV last night. It was _____ than *Star Dogs 1*.

B. | Objective Pronouns | **Write sentences.**

1. for / you / will / me / some / make / cookies

   _____

2. shoelaces / can / his / I / for / tie / him

   _____

3. to / park / come / me / the / with

   _____

Unit 10

| Comparative and Superlative Adjectives | **Write sentences. *Use more . . . than* and *the most*. Use the adjectives in the box.**

| difficult   exciting   dangerous   interesting |

1. It's _____ to paint pictures.

2. It's _____ to play sports.

3. Meg wants to be an artist. It's _____ job.

Antonyms

An antonym is a word that has a meaning opposite from another word.

A. Find and circle the antonyms for the words in the box.

cold	easy	early	small	short
sad	old	fast	pretty	run

```
w f (h o t) u y r c y l v u o s
w m m n a e w c m j l a z e l
g b i g l w y o u n g g r b o
h h l t l a k r g b j r u g w
a o j s o l a j l y h n b h e
r q w a n k f j y s z l s t a
d d i f f i c u l t c n o g z
y h r r v z v z c y z o g n w
d k h a p p y a z t z m k i n
v m t q k m b y v l a t e r r
```

B. Write the pairs of antonyms.

cold   hot   _____ _____

_____ _____   _____ _____

_____ _____   _____ _____

_____ _____   _____ _____

_____ _____   _____ _____

Prefixes

A prefix changes the meaning of a word.

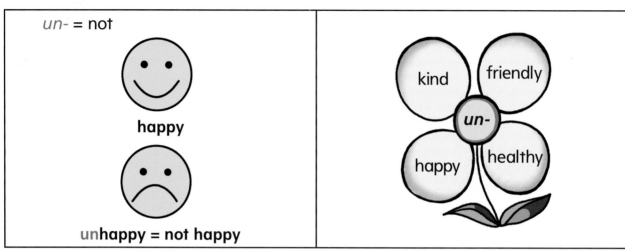

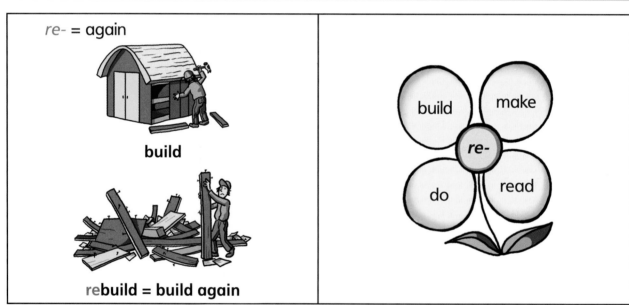

Complete the sentences with words with prefixes.

1. Jon read a book to his sister yesterday. He is going to _____ it today.

2. They couldn't put out the fire. Now they have to _____ the house.

3. Take care of your pets. Don't be _____ to them.

4. Mike couldn't catch a ball at the game. He was very _____.

5. The cookies smelled bad. The children had to _____ them.

6. Don't pet that dog. It looks _____.

Suffixes

A suffix changes the part of speech.

Write the new words.

-er = person who

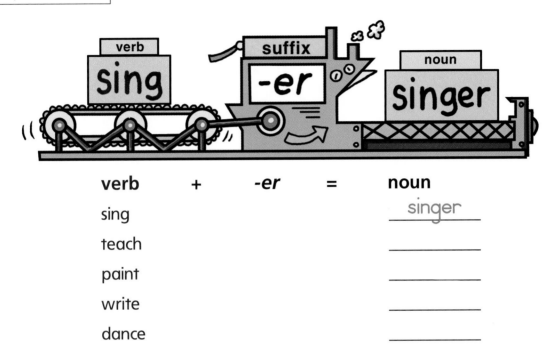

verb	+	-er	=	noun
sing				singer
teach				_____
paint				_____
write				_____
dance				_____

-ly = in a certain way

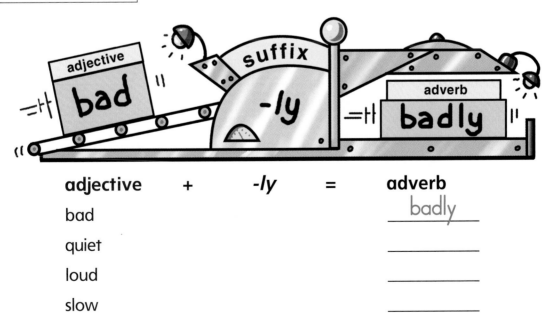

adjective	+	-ly	=	adverb
bad				badly
quiet				_____
loud				_____
slow				_____

The Senses

Complete the lists with words in the box.

beautiful	delicious	ears	eyes	fingers
hear	loud	nose	see	smell
soft	sour	taste	tongue	touch

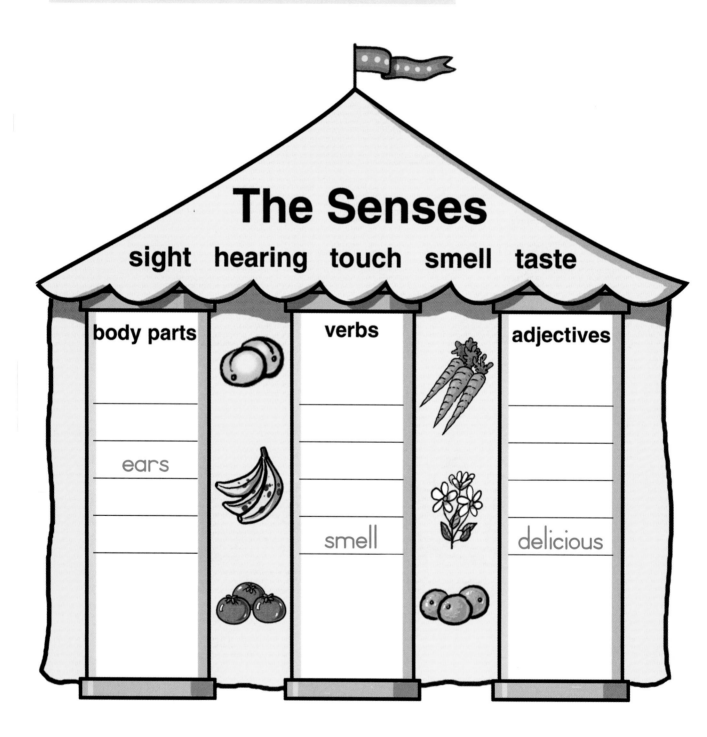

The Senses

sight hearing touch smell taste

body parts

ears

verbs

smell

adjectives

delicious

Word List

act in movies

angry

artist

astronaut

athlete

bag of sugar

basket

be kind

best (runner)

biggest (animal)

bowl

cabinet

catch (the ball)

chores

climb (the tree)

dancer

(a) cold

dark (hair)

collect dolls

do experiments

collect stamps

draw pictures

container (of milk)

drive a truck

curly

excited

dance

firefighter

headache

loaf of bread

help

longest (neck)

hungry

look for insects

hurts

make jewelry

ice cream

meet friends

jar

movie star

juicy

musician

nervous

older than

paint pictures

park

photographer

plant a garden

play the guitar

play sports

play tennis

put out fires

refrigerator

scared

scientist

sew

share (my toys)

shelf

shiny

shortest (tail)

(feels) sick

sing on stage

singer

smell (the flowers)

soft

sore throat

stomachache

straight (hair)

take out the garbage

take photographs

tallest (boy)

thirsty

tie shoelaces

tired

toothache

travel in space

truck driver

use a computer

wash clothes

water the plants

wear a dress

worst (weather)

writer

younger than